blue note

The Jazz
Photographs of
FRANCIS
WOLFF

a book of postcards

Pomegranate

SAN FRANCISCO

Pomegranate
Box 6099
Rohnert Park, CA 94927

Pomegranate Europe Ltd.
Fullbridge House, Fullbridge
Maldon, Essex CM9 7LE
England

ISBN 1-56640-021-X
Pomegranate Catalog No. A607

Pomegranate publishes books of
postcards on a wide range of subjects.
Please write to the publisher for more information.

Cover design by Elizabeth Key
Printed in Korea
05 04 03 02 01 00 99 98 97 96   12 11 10 9 8 7 6 5 4 3

Nobody has ever documented an era more lovingly, or more thoroughly, than Blue Note Records founders Alfred Lion and Francis (Frank) Wolff. The era that they chronicled: the inception and rise of bebop in America.

Lion's charge was the music. He recorded a staggering array of seminal jazz artists from 1939 through 1967. Wolff's contribution to history was more subtle but no less significant. Using a hand-held Leica or Rolleiflex camera, he, too, recorded every Blue Note artist for posterity. Yet Francis Wolff never considered himself an archivist. He took pictures simply because he loved doing it.

Even during the days of 78s in plain paper sleeves, before there appeared to be any use for his photographs, Wolff and his camera were an ubiquitous presence at every Blue Note session. Whether attempting to fade into the wallpaper or blatantly seeking out the perfect combination of light, angle, and expression to capture an artist's spirit, Francis Wolff never missed an opportunity to indulge his two passions in life—music and photography.

With the dawning of the LP, new possibilities for graphic innovation arose, and three hundred of Francis Wolff's jazz photographs were artfully cropped, integrated with typography, and given jazz immortality as Blue Note album covers. More than five thousand others went into a file drawer, not to see the light of day until twenty years after Wolff's death.

With Wolff's passing in 1971, his entire collection of priceless photographs went to his Blue Note partner and childhood friend, Alfred Lion. For years, Lion could not bear to go near them. It was only when Lion formed a warm friendship with the principals of Mosaic Records that anyone outside the original Blue Note family became aware that this treasure trove of Francis Wolff photographs still existed.

Mosaic Records has set aside the photographs most appropriate for use in its continuing program of Blue Note reissues. Aside from the album reissues and Mosaic Records brochures, this book of postcards marks the first appearance of a selection of Francis Wolff Blue Note photographs in twenty-five years.

blue note

THE JAZZ PHOTOGRAPHS OF FRANCIS WOLFF

Curtis Fuller
Art Blakey's *Buhaina's Delight* session
Englewood Cliffs, New Jersey, December 18, 1961

POMEGRANATE BOX 6099 ROHNERT PARK CA 94927

THELONIOUS MONK, NEW YORK, 1948
PHOTOGRAPH BY © WILLIAM P. GOTTLIEB

M139

ISBN 1881270629

7 48053 02755 0

fotofolio.com

blue note
THE JAZZ PHOTOGRAPHS OF FRANCIS WOLFF

Ron Carter
Joe Henderson's *Mode for Joe* session
Englewood Cliffs, New Jersey, January 27, 1966

POMEGRANATE BOX 6099 ROHNERT PARK CA 94927

blue note

THE JAZZ PHOTOGRAPHS OF FRANCIS WOLFF

Lou Donaldson, Clifford Brown, and Elmo Hope
Donaldson-Brown Quintet session
WOR Studios, New York, New York, June 9, 1953

POMEGRANATE   BOX 6099   ROHNERT PARK, CA 94927

blue note
THE JAZZ PHOTOGRAPHS OF FRANCIS WOLFF

Sonny Clark
Leapin' & Lopin' session
Englewood Cliffs, New Jersey, November 13, 1961

POMEGRANATE   BOX 6099   ROHNERT PARK CA 94927

blue note
THE JAZZ PHOTOGRAPHS OF FRANCIS WOLFF

Kenny Drew
Undercurrent session
Englewood Cliffs, New Jersey, December 11, 1960

POMEGRANATE BOX 6099 ROHNERT PARK CA 94927

blue note

THE JAZZ PHOTOGRAPHS OF FRANCIS WOLFF

Grant Green
Rejected session
Englewood Cliffs, New Jersey, November 26, 1960

POMEGRANATE BOX 6099 ROHNERT PARK CA 94927

blue note
THE JAZZ PHOTOGRAPHS OF FRANCIS WOLFF

Lee Morgan
Johnny Griffin's *A Blowing Session*
Hackensack, New Jersey, April 6, 1957

POMEGRANATE   BOX 6099   ROHNERT PARK, CA 94927

blue note

THE JAZZ PHOTOGRAPHS OF FRANCIS WOLFF

Hank Mobley
Donald Byrd's *Byrd in Flight* session
Englewood Cliffs, New Jersey, January 17, 1960

POMEGRANATE BOX 6099 ROHNERT PARK CA 94927

blue note
THE JAZZ PHOTOGRAPHS OF FRANCIS WOLFF

Thad Jones
The Magnificent Thad Jones session
Hackensack, New Jersey, February 2, 1957

POMEGRANATE BOX 6099 ROHNERT PARK CA 94927

blue note

THE JAZZ PHOTOGRAPHS OF FRANCIS WOLFF

Andrew Hill
Involution session
Englewood Cliffs, New Jersey, March 7, 1966

POMEGRANATE BOX 6099 ROHNERT PARK CA 94927

blue note
THE JAZZ PHOTOGRAPHS OF FRANCIS WOLFF

Elvin Jones
Grant Green's *Talkin' About* session
Englewood Cliffs, New Jersey, September 11, 1964

POMEGRANATE BOX 6099 ROHNERT PARK CA 94927

blue note
THE JAZZ PHOTOGRAPHS OF FRANCIS WOLFF

Freddie Hubbard
Hank Mobley's *The Turnaround!* session
Englewood Cliffs, New Jersey, February 5, 1965

Pomegranate Box 6099 Rohnert Park, CA 94927

blue note
THE JAZZ PHOTOGRAPHS OF FRANCIS WOLFF

Sonny Rollins
Sonny Rollins Volume II session
Hackensack, New Jersey, April 14, 1957

POMEGRANATE   BOX 6099   ROHNERT PARK, CA 94927

blue note

THE JAZZ PHOTOGRAPHS OF FRANCIS WOLFF

Herbie Hancock
Wayne Shorter's *Speak No Evil* session
Englewood Cliffs, New Jersey, December 24, 1964

POMEGRANATE BOX 6099 ROHNERT PARK CA 94927

blue note

THE JAZZ PHOTOGRAPHS OF FRANCIS WOLFF

Joe Henderson
Mode for Joe session
Englewood Cliffs, New Jersey, January 27, 1966

POMEGRANATE BOX 6099 ROHNERT PARK CA 94927

© Mosaic Images

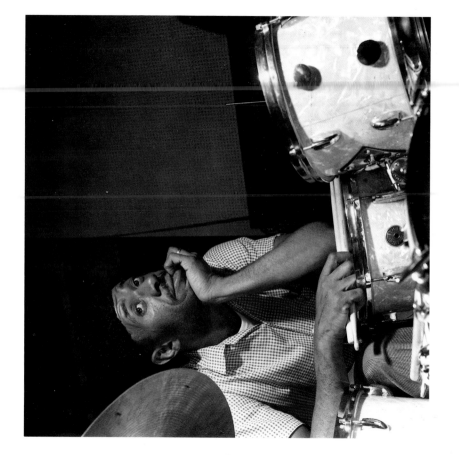

blue note

THE JAZZ PHOTOGRAPHS OF FRANCIS WOLFF

Philly Joe Jones
Kenny Dorham's *Whistle Stop* session
Englewood Cliffs, New Jersey, January 15, 1961

POMEGRANATE BOX 6099 ROHNERT PARK CA 94927

blue note
THE JAZZ PHOTOGRAPHS OF FRANCIS WOLFF

Ornette Coleman
The Empty Foxhole session
Englewood Cliffs, New Jersey, September 9, 1966

POMEGRANATE   BOX 6099   ROHNERT PARK, CA 94927

blue note
THE JAZZ PHOTOGRAPHS OF FRANCIS WOLFF

Sam Jones
Grant Green's *Oleo* session
Englewood Cliffs, New Jersey, January 31, 1962

POMEGRANATE   BOX 6099   ROHNERT PARK CA 94927

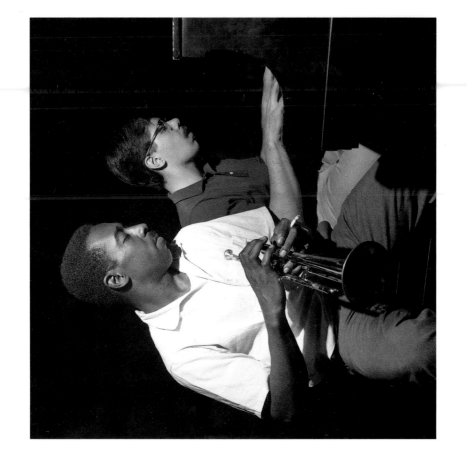

blue note

THE JAZZ PHOTOGRAPHS OF FRANCIS WOLFF

Blue Mitchell and Chick Corea
Blue Mitchell's *The Thing to Do* session
Englewood Cliffs, New Jersey, July 30, 1964

POMEGRANATE BOX 6099 ROHNERT PARK CA 94927

blue note

THE JAZZ PHOTOGRAPHS OF FRANCIS WOLFF

Joe Henderson and Bobby Hutcherson
Grant Green's *Idle Moments* session
Englewood Cliffs, New Jersey,
November 4 or November 15, 1963

POMEGRANATE BOX 6099 ROHNERT PARK CA 94927

blue note
THE JAZZ PHOTOGRAPHS OF FRANCIS WOLFF

Bud Powell
The Scene Changes session
Hackensack, New Jersey, December 29, 1958

POMEGRANATE BOX 6099 ROHNERT PARK, CA 94927

blue note
THE JAZZ PHOTOGRAPHS OF FRANCIS WOLFF

Paul Chambers
Sonny Rollins Volume II session
Hackensack, New Jersey, April 14, 1957

POMEGRANATE   BOX 6099   ROHNERT PARK, CA 94927

blue note

THE JAZZ PHOTOGRAPHS OF FRANCIS WOLFF

Doug Watkins and Horace Silver
Horace Silver Quintet session
Hackensack, New Jersey, February 6, 1955

POMEGRANATE   BOX 6099   ROHNERT PARK CA 94927

© Mosaic Images

blue note

THE JAZZ PHOTOGRAPHS OF FRANCIS WOLFF

Kenny Clarke, Milt Jackson, Percy Heath, and John Lewis
In performance
New York, New York, April 1952

POMEGRANATE BOX 6099 ROHNERT PARK CA 94927

blue note

THE JAZZ PHOTOGRAPHS OF FRANCIS WOLFF

Junior Cook
Blue Mitchell's *Boss Horn* session
Englewood Cliffs, New Jersey, November 17, 1966

POMEGRANATE BOX 6099 ROHNERT PARK CA 94927